D0897253

YOU CAN BE HEALED

God Still Heals Today

YOU CAN BE HEALED

God Still Heals Today

BOB GASS

with Ruth Gass Halliday

You Can Be Healed

DEDICATION

*This book is dedicated to
Doctor Joseph S. Wilson, Jr., M.D., F.A.C.C.,*

*Thank you for listening and allowing God to use
you — just when I needed it most!*

YOU CAN BE HEALED:
God Still Heals Today
Copyright ©2002 by Bob Gass
Library of Congress Catalog Number: pending
International Standard Book Number: 1-931727-08-02

SYNERGY PUBLISHERS
Gainesville, Florida 32635

TABLE OF CONTENTS

1
NINETY PERCENT BLOCKAGE

While writing this book I discovered I had a *ninety-percent blockage* in a main coronary artery.

Early last year I began to experience shortness of breath and sporadic chest discomfort. So I went to my insurance company cardiologist, who administered a treadmill stress test, and gave me the "all clear."

However, by the end of the year I was having even more of the same symptoms.

A voice within me (*one I've learned to listen to!*) prompted me to contact Doctor Joseph Wilson, Jr., a leading cardiologist in the southeast, and have him perform a heart catheter test. During this procedure dye is injected into the veins through a main artery in the groin, allowing the doctor to view the coronary arteries on a screen. As tests go, it's considered to be "the gold standard."

However, because Doctor Wilson was not a participating physician in my particular health insurance plan, I went back to the cardiologist who'd administered my original treadmill test.

After carefully explaining my family history of heart disease, my symptoms, and my concerns, I requested a heart catheter test.

But he refused.

"It's invasive," he said, "We only do it in extreme circumstances." (I wondered *what* would be considered "extreme circumstances," but I didn't ask!)

He administered yet another treadmill stress test, and said everything looked okay.

John the Apostle writes, "Ye have an unction from the holy one and ye *know* all things" (1 Jn 2:20). There are things you "know," that you can neither document nor explain. That's because they are made known to you by God's Spirit. I call this *divine intuition* – and I've learned to trust it.

Even though a highly-respected physician had told me that treadmill tests are ninety-five to ninety-seven percent reliable, I still didn't have peace; and I believe we are to be "led…with peace" (Isa 55:12).

Paul writes, "Let the peace of God rule in your hearts" (Col 3:15). The word *rule* literally means, "to umpire." Just as an umpire makes the call, ruling in favor of one side or the other, so God's peace – or the lack of it – should determine what we *do* and *don't* do.

Again the voice within me urged, "Go see Doctor Wilson and have him do a heart catheter test.

Finally I did!

I explained to him that my dad had died at age forty-four of coronary thrombosis, my mum at age seventy-four of a massive heart attack, and that my brother Neil, who is just two years older than me, had required angioplasty for a heart blockage nine years ago.

Dr. Wilson agreed to do the test early the following Monday morning. Later that afternoon he came into my hospital room holding a picture of my arteries.

Looking at me intently, he said, *"The Spirit of God certainly led you. I'm glad you persevered in spite of the opinions you were given. You have a ninety-percent blockage in one of the main arteries carrying blood to your heart. You could have gone for the next five years and not had a problem, or you could have had a heart attack within the next five days."*

The following day I underwent angioplasty, a simple procedure using a small "balloon" to open the blocked artery, and implanting a "stent" to keep it open. On Wednesday I was back home, feeling extremely grateful to God for leading me, knowing I'd just experienced a miracle of divine intervention.

Listen to these words: "His sheep follow him because they know his voice" (Jn 10:4 NIV). Learn to *listen* to the voice of God within you – your life could depend on it!

And it *is* something you have to *learn*.

I've spent forty-plus years in the ministry, and I *still* struggle at times wondering, "Is this *God* speaking, or is it just me?" I've come to understand that I'll *always* face that challenge – and so will you. But the good news is, the closer you get to Him the easier it is to discern His voice.

Do you believe that when you pray, God will answer?

If you do, your answer can come in several ways. (1) Through the Scriptures. (2) Through circumstances. (3) Through the wise counsel of others. (4) Through the voice of God within you.

That's why it's so important to take time to *listen, recognize,* and *respond* to His voice.

2
THE CHOICE IS YOURS!

One of the first miracle's I ever witnessed was at an old-fashioned tent meeting with evangelist, Oral Roberts. I watched him remove the iron braces from the legs of a four-year-old polio victim. After laying hands on the little guy and praying for him, Oral walked to the far side of the platform, opened his arms wide and shouted, "Run for Jesus!"

Suddenly, a child who could barely walk with the aid of awkward metal braces, *ran* across the stage and leapt up into his arms. In tears, Oral asked him, "Who did it?" Without hesitation the child answered, *"Jesus did it! Jesus did it!"*

Moved by this demonstration of God's power, hundreds of people came forward that night to commit their lives to Christ.

Thirty years later I interviewed Oral and asked him about what had happened that night.

He told me, "Bob, that little fellow's now a Dad, and he *still* runs and plays ball with his kids."

Then I asked him, "Do you have any idea how many people you've laid hands on during your ministry?"

"My biographers reckon over a million," he replied.

"How many of them were healed?" I asked.

"The people who do the follow-up estimate about two or three-percent."

"What about the other ninety-seven-per-cent?" I asked.

"That's the *first* question I'm going to ask Jesus when I get to heaven," he replied with a big smile.

Then he grew serious and said, "Bob, you've only two options. Option one, *don't* pray for the sick, and *don't* believe God for miracles. That way you'll never be criticized. Option two, *build* people's faith by preaching God's Word to them. Lay hands on the sick, as Jesus told us to, and believe that they'll recover."

Then his gaze narrowed and he looked at me intently. "Bob," he said, *"You can do one or the other – but you can't do both!"*

Right there and then I made a choice to: (a) stand on The Word of the One who said, "I am the Lord that healeth thee" (Ex 15:26); (b) pray in *faith* expecting results, because Jesus said, "Whatever things you ask when you pray, believe that you receive them, and you will have them" (Mk 11:24 NKJV); (c) join in prayerful agreement with the leaders of any local church, because the Bible says, "Is anyone among you sick? Let him call for the elders of the church, and let them pray over him, anointing him with oil in the name of the Lord. And the prayer of faith will save the sick, and the Lord will raise him up" (Jas 5:4-15 NKJV).

It's not *my* responsibility to heal anyone! It's my job to introduce them to Jesus, who "…healed *all* who were sick, that it might be fulfilled which was spoken by Isaiah the prophet, saying; 'He himself *took* our infirmities and *bore* our sicknesses'" (Mt 8:16-17 NKJV).

How come Paul raised Eutychus from the dead (Ac 20:9), and yet wrote, "Trophimus I have left in Miletus sick?" (2 Ti 4:20 NKJV). And why did he instruct Timothy, "Use a little wine for your stomach's sake and your frequent infir-

mities" (1 Ti 5:23 NKJV), instead of simply praying for him? Had Paul *already* prayed and nothing changed?

I don't know!

How come Elisha did *twice* as many miracles
as his boss Elijah, yet he became, "… sick with
the illness of which he would die" (2 Ki 13:14
NKJV).

I don't know!

Maybe his assignment on earth was complete, and we all die from *something*.

Here's the score; if you're looking for a reason to *doubt*, you'll find it among those who sin-
cerely believe that the day of miracles is past. But
if you're looking for reasons to *believe*, you'll find
them from one end of the Bible to the other.

The choice is yours.

I choose to believe the God who says, "I am
the Lord, I change not" (Mal 3:6). What does
that mean? It means: (a) His *compassion* toward
us never changes, it's "new every morning"
(La 3:23). (b) His *power* to heal us never
changes, He is "the same yesterday, and today,
and forever" (Heb 13:5).

(c) His *Word* never changes, He said, "If you

abide in Me and My words abide in you, you will ask what you desire and it shall be done for you" (Jn 15:7 NKJV).

So what *does* the Bible teach about healing? Read on and find out!

3
A TESTIMONY OF HEALING

Dr. Victor Pearce is not only my friend, he's also an ordained minister, and an *Oxford* scholar. When I requested permission to share with you the story of his remarkable healing, he sent me the following e-mail:

"Bob Gass has kindly asked me to give the details as to how I was healed from a serious *heart condition* at the age of *nineteen*. It illustrates how God has given *specific* gifts of healing to particular persons, as distinct from the *general* promise of healing granted to a church of praying people.

"I had just switched from Applied Science and Engineering at London University to prepare for entrance exams at a theological college, and the studies were quite intense.

"I went to see Dr. Grierson because I had *fainted* several times. He examined me and said,

'You have a serious heart condition, and if you don't give up your studies immediately and take to bed, I'm afraid the consequences could be bad!'

"He told me to report back to him in a week's time.

"The day before I was due to visit him again, I attended a meeting which was being held by Pastor George Jeffreys. Those who needed healing were invited to come for 'the laying on of hands,' so I went forward and he laid his hands on my head.

"I felt better immediately.

"The next day I reported to Dr. Grierson as arranged, and he gave me a thorough exam. Looking more and more astonished, he said, *'I can't understand what has happened to you. All symptoms of heart failure have disappeared! Forget my instructions, go home and lead a normal life.'*

"This I did, and here I am at age *eighty-eight* to tell you that God did a thorough job!"

Dr. Pearce continues, "My healing illustrates that God does give a special *gift* of healing to particular believers, as explained in 1 Corinthians 12:9. The Jeffreys brothers were one example. A particular characteristic of their healings was that they were usually *immediate*, as in my case.

"They had been given this gift quite suddenly a little time before.

"It seems to me that this was in order to meet special needs which would arise at the outbreak of the First World War. I tell the story in my book, *Miracles and Angels* (Eagle Books, Guilford).

"At the meeting where I was healed, George Jeffreys shared a remarkable vision which had appeared to his brother, Stephen, on Sunday, July 21, 1914, as he was preaching at a service in Llanelly, South Wales.

"Stephen could see that the congregation's attention was riveted in his direction, but not on him.

Puzzled, he came down from the platform to see what they were pointing to, and to his amazement, he saw on the wall behind where he'd been standing, the image of a lamb. After a few minutes it changed into the face of Christ. It was a living face, because people could quite clearly see his eyelids flicker. His hair was streaked with white, so that He looked like a middle-aged man, stricken with grief.

"Then the image changed back again into the head of a lamb. It was alive and moving, and after a few minutes it was again transformed into the living, moving, face of Christ, with beautiful tears rolling down His cheeks. This indeed was the "Man of sorrows," the One who bore our *griefs*, and by whose stripes we were *healed* (See Isa 53:3-7).

"Pastor Jeffreys had been preaching on the text, 'That I may know Him… and the fellowship of his suffering' (Php 3:10).

"He began to appeal to his listeners to respond to that love by forsaking their sins and receiving forgiveness. During his appeal, the face of the Man of sorrows became enshrouded in glory.

"One onlooker described it as, 'Most beautiful beyond description, kindly beyond words. And the eyes! They looked at you personally –loving, sad, and glorious eyes, which moved in the living face.'

"George Jeffreys told us how long this vision lasted.

It was not just for a brief time; long after the meeting finished it was still there. It lasted through the night and into the morning. As news spread throughout the town, hundreds flocked to see it for themselves, and hear yet another message from the evangelist.

"Of course some tried to explain it away.

One man went to the wall and tried unsuccessfully to wipe it off. Another, a painter and decorator, took a cloth and held it over the vision, but to his surprise it shone right through. Yet another attempted to rationalize it by saying it was a hallucination, caused by a flickering electric light. Stephen Jeffreys did not argue; He merely turned off the light, and there, still shining, was the Savior's face, even more living and real.

"Another man thought the bright light was shining through some sort of stained glass window. But when Stephen tested that theory by having the blinds drawn and excluding all light, it made no difference. The vision continued to shine.

"As news of it continued to blaze around the town, all kinds of people came to see it – all ages and types, tradesmen, professionals, alcoholics and people with other problems.

"Little did they know that within *two weeks* the whole world would change forever. The world's worst war would break out, and *hundreds* of those young men who'd filed in to see the vision and have their doubts changed to faith, would shed their blood in the fields of Flanders."

"So, Bob," Victor wrote, "I gladly share with you and your readers that at age *nineteen* I was written off to die. But God had something else in mind, and here I am almost *seventy years later,* still writing books and broadcasting the gospel!"

4
INSTRUCTIONS FOR HEALING

Before you can truly exercise faith for healing you need to know what the Scriptures teach about it.

Paul writes, "Faith cometh [grows] by hearing, and hearing by the word of God" (Ro 10:17). The Bible is "faith food." It causes your faith to increase, and enables you to believe God for progressively greater things.

The story is told of an American tourist who visited a small Irish village, and asked a local farmer, "Were there any great men born in this town?" The farmer replied, "Nope, just babies!"

We *all* start as spiritual babies, and go from grade to grade in the school of faith. In this school there's only one teacher – The Holy Spirit. And only one textbook – the Bible. And you never graduate. You're *always* learning; *always* bringing your mind into harmony with the mind of God as revealed in the Scriptures.

The *hand* of faith can't take from God what the *eye* of faith can't see to be the will of God.

Instead of saying, "Pray for me," you should first say, "Teach me God's Word so that I can intelligently cooperate in my own recovery."

Proverbs 4:20-22 gives us instructions on how to receive healing: "*Attend* to my words; incline thine *ear* unto my sayings. Let them not depart from thine *eyes*; keep them in the midst of thine *heart*. For they are life unto those that *find* them, and *health* to all their flesh."

The Word of God can't bring *health* to you until you (a) hear it; (b) accept it; (c) apply it. Before you can receive anything from God, you must take the time to "find" what He promises. That means having:

An attentive ear. "Incline thine ear unto my sayings."

A steadfast look. "Let them not depart from thine eyes."

An accepting heart. "Keep them in the midst of thine heart."

Paul writes, "It is with your heart that you believe…and it is with your mouth that you confess" (Ro 10:10 NIV).

Here's a timeless formula you need to apply in your daily life: *Conviction + confession = results!*

When somebody asks, "How can you justify believing such a thing?" Your answer should be, *"Because I agree with the God who promised it."*

Conviction without confession is like faith without works – it's dead. And confession without conviction is just empty words. But put the two together and you begin to get results!

Many of us *hide* our convictions because we're afraid of being criticized. It's when you "put it out there" that the battle really begins. The enemy knows that when your mouth speaks what your heart believes, mountains are moved, giants are toppled, circumstances are changed, and sickness is healed.

You don't need a penny in your pocket, a friend on the phone, or a contact in high places for God to move on your behalf. You simply need to:

(1) *Take ownership of God's promises.* Believe in your heart that they're yours!

(2) *Work on your faith.* Go through the necessary faith-training in small areas before you

attempt to conquer in big ones.

(3) *Develop your spiritual muscles.* Resistance is good, because it requires divine assistance. When you've nothing left but God, you'll discover – God is enough!

(4) *Persevere.* Sometimes the only way out is through. Trials are God's training ground for bigger victories ahead.

David prayed, "Do as you promised…that your name will be great forever" (1 Ch 17:23-24 NIV). When you know God well enough to say "do as you promised," things begin to change.

Faith is not "psyching" yourself up. Actually, it's only as good as the object in which you place it. Faith in a broken bridge won't get you across the river – but faith in the God who says, "I am watching to see that my word is fulfilled" will! (See Jer 1:12 NIV).

Reminding God of His promise is like presenting a check issued to you from His account, and endorsed with His signature. *Whose account? God's!* Whose signature? *God's!* Paul says, "He *always* does exactly what he says. He carries out and fulfills *all*…promises, no matter how many of them there are" (2 Co 1:19 TLB).

We make promises we can't keep, and people get hurt – but not God! He's never broken one yet!

Why then don't we see more of them fulfilled?

Because they're conditional! If you follow His instructions, you'll get what He promised, because: (1) His *truth* won't allow Him to deceive you. (2) His *integrity* won't allow Him to renege on His Word to you. (3) His *grace* won't allow Him to forget you.

But before you can pray, "Lord, do as you promised" you've got to *know* what He *promised*.

Among those who sought healing during Christ's earthly ministry, we read of only one – a leper – who said, "Lord, if thou *wilt*, thou canst make me clean" (Lk 5:12). The first thing Jesus did was correct his theology by saying, "I *will*, be thou clean" (Lk 5:13). Christ's "I will," cancelled the man's "if." No one ever looked in vain to The Great Physician!

Listen carefully to these Scriptures:

"And Jesus went about all Galilee teaching …preaching the gospel…and healing *all manner* of sickness and *all manner* of disease…they brought unto him all sick people that were taken with [diverse] diseases…and he healed them *all*" (Mt 4:23-24).

Listen again: "When he saw the multitudes, he was moved with compassion on them…. And when he had called unto him his twelve disciples, he gave *them* power…to heal *all* manner of sickness…" (Mt 9:36 & 10:1).

As His fame spread and the crowds became larger, Jesus *empowered* His twelve disciples to go out and heal the sick; then He sent seventy more to do the same thing.

His desire is to *reproduce* Himself through us!

Listen, "Verily, verily, I say unto you, He that believeth on me, the works that I do shall he do also; and greater works than these shall he do; because I go unto my Father. And whatsoever ye shall ask in my name, that will I do, that the Father may be glorified" (Jn 14:12-13).

Miraculous healings were a regular occurrence in The New Testament church. Listen, "Through the hands of the apostles many signs and wonders were done among the people…they brought the sick out into the streets and laid them on beds and couches, that at least the shadow of Peter passing by might fall on some of them. Also a multitude gathered from the surrounding cities to Jerusalem, bringing sick people and those who were tormented by unclean spirits, and they were *all* healed" (Ac 5:12-16 NKJV).

The Holy Spirit, whom Jesus sent as His successor and executive, took possession of the church, which is the body of Christ, and demonstrated the *same* healing power that Christ had displayed during His earthly ministry. In The Gospels, as in The Acts, we never read of *anyone* asking for healing and being denied.

Men named this book *The Acts of the Apostles*, but a more accurate name might be *The Acts of the Holy Spirit* as He worked through ordinary people like us.

Dr. Jim McConnell, who pastors the three-thousand-member Metropolitan Tabernacle in Belfast, Northern Ireland, told me of a forty-eight year-old woman who attended one of his Tuesday morning *healing clinics*.

She was in the final stages of cancer, and the doctors gave her no hope.

Jim laid hands on her, prayed for her, and unexpectedly heard himself saying, "After three days the Lord will raise you up again."

The next day she collapsed on the street and was taken into the Intensive Care Unit, where she was placed on life support. On Friday, three days after she'd been prayed for, the hospital called her family in and took her off life support, expecting she would die.

But she didn't.

When they removed the equipment, she sat up in bed and asked, *"Where am I?"*

Today this woman's alive, cancer-free, and healthy.

5
SPEAKING THE WORD!

Eric Martin was healed over *a one-year period,* as he thought about, meditated on, and confessed God's promises.

After smoking three packs a day for thirty years, Eric had committed his life to Christ. With his conversion came an ability he'd never had before – the power to quit smoking. He didn't know such joy was possible!

But he was battling emphysema, and some days, especially when the pollen count was high, he'd spend hours wearing a facemask and breathing oxygen from a portable tank.

He'd been anointed with oil (a symbol of The Holy Spirit), and the elders of his local church had laid hands on him and prayed "the prayer of faith," believing for his healing. (See James 5:14).

Daily Eric confessed God's Word, by saying,

"Lord, Your Word says that:

(1) You'll forgive *all* of my iniquities and heal *all* of my diseases (See Ps 103:3).

(2) You'll take sickness away from me, and fulfill the length of my days (See Ex 23:25-26).

(3) You *took* my infirmity and *bore* my sickness, and by Your stripes I'm healed (See Isa 53:5).

(4) You'll restore health to me and heal me of my wounds (See Jer 30:17).

(5) No plague will come near my dwelling; I can call upon You and You'll will answer me, You'll be with me in trouble, You'll honor me, deliver me, and satisfy me with long life (See Ps 91).

If I abide in You and Your words abide in me, I can ask for what I need and it will be given to me (See Jn 15:7)."

Some days his words seemed to *mock* him – especially when he was fighting for each breath.

But he kept believing, and confessing "I'm not moved by what I *see*, and I'm not moved by what I *feel*. I'm moved by what I *believe*, and I believe that by Your stripes I'm *healed*. So until my symptoms line up with Your word, I'll believe You and nothing else."

Many of Eric's friends smiled indulgently,

quietly questioned his sanity, and described him in psychological terms.

But he remained steadfast!

He understood he couldn't depend on his *senses*, because the things of God can't be discerned, or appropriated by our *natural* minds. Physical sensations like pain, weakness, and sickness are never valid reasons for doubting God's Word.

He was greatly encouraged one Sunday morning when his pastor, speaking about Abram, said, "God told Abram 'I will make you the father of many nations.'" Even though he was almost one-hundred years old, and his wife, ninety, God changed his name from Abram to *Abraham*, which means *"the father of a multitude."*

For the next twenty years Abraham wore that prophetic name, and went about 'confessing' God's promise! Can you imagine what his friends must have thought?

Eric's pastor read these words: "Without weakening in his faith, he [Abraham] faced the fact that his body was as good as dead...*yet he did not waiver* through unbelief regarding the promise of God, but was strengthened in his faith and gave glory to God, being *fully persuaded* that God had power to do what he had promised" (Ro 4:19-21 NIV).

How is such faith possible?

Because Abraham believed that God "gives life to the dead and calls those things which do not exist as though they did" (Ro 4:17 NKJV).

On the other hand look at Peter.

The waves were just as high when he walked on top of them as they were when he sank. As long as he didn't focus on them they couldn't hinder him, but the minute he did, he began to sink.

As long as you're preoccupied with *looking* and *feeling*, instead of *standing* on God's Word and *refusing* to doubt, you can't receive what He wants to give you!

The Bible says, "Hold fast what you have" (Rev 3:11 NKJV).

Why? Because Satan will try to *take* from you everything that God's given you. Jesus gave Peter the power to walk on water, but the enemy took it from him by getting him to fix his attention on the wind (*what we feel*), and on the waves (*what we see*).

Peter had power and he used it; but as soon as he began to focus on his surroundings instead of keeping his eyes on Jesus, he lost it.

You can *lose* a healing already in progress by directing your focus away from The Word of God and on to your symptoms and feelings!

"But how can I say I'm healed when I still see evidence of disease in my body, and I still have pain?" you ask.

Maybe this illustration will help.

One method of killing a tree is to *girdle* it, by removing a ring of bark from around the trunk. When that happens, it's as good as dead. Yet for a while its foliage is as fresh and green as ever, and the tree continues to show every sign of life. But the master gardener, whose knowledge and experience is greater than ours, *sees* the end result. He knows that in time the leaves will wither and fall, and the death of the tree will become apparent to all.

So it is when we claim healing.

We stand squarely on The Word of God, believing that the sword of the Spirit strikes a deathblow to our sickness. For a while the symptoms may remain – and in some cases even appear to get worse. But the eye of faith *sees* disease destroyed and health restored, and the voice of faith keeps *calling* those things that are *not* as though they *were*, until sickness disappears and healing is manifested.

John writes, "The Word was God" (Jn 1:1). That means that every time you absorb God's Word, you're absorbing more of God. Can you imagine what *that* does to sickness, habits, depression, and any other destructive force at work in your life?

God said, "So shall My word be that goes forth from My mouth. It shall not return to Me void, but it shall *accomplish* what I please, And it shall *prosper* in the thing for which I sent it" (Isa 55:11 NKJV).

David wrote, "He *sent* his word, and healed them, and delivered them from their destructions" (Ps 107:20).

Paul writes, "The word is near you; it is in your *mouth* and in your *heart*; that is, the word of faith we are proclaiming" (Ro 10:8 NIV).

The enemy doesn't fear your sin; he knows God can forgive it. He doesn't fear your depression; he knows God can drive it away. He doesn't fear your poverty; he knows God can provide. *He fears your discovery of God's Word, because your ignorance of it is the most effective weapon he can use against you when you're sick.*

After one full year of confessing God's Word *in spite* of his symptoms, his emotions, his reason, his prognosis, and the opinions of his friends, Eric Martin's doctor was amazed at the change. So amazed, in fact, that he referred him to a prominent specialist to find out what was going on.

Two weeks later the specialist issued a report saying, "Eric's lungs are completely healthy and functional – *they're the lungs of a man half his age!"*

6
You Must Be Diligent!

What if Eric Martin had given up in *six*, or even *eleven* months, and said, "This just isn't working?"

Listen carefully, "Without faith it is impossible to please him: For he that cometh to God must believe that he is, and that he is a rewarder of them that *diligently* seek him" (Heb 11:6).

The word *diligent* means *painstaking and persevering*. Does that describe you?

We hear a lot about the *promises*, but not much about the *process*. Yet it's in the process that we get discouraged and quit. That's because we've become a bunch of fair-weather, Johnny-come-lately, microwave Christians!

Success in any venture lies in holding on, even when others let go. We want instant gratification, and when we don't get it we leave our jobs, our churches, and even our families.

There's a process you must go through, and it requires *diligence*! There are no shortcuts. You've got to pay full price – it never goes on sale!

Endurance is the price tag for victory.

Listen, "We pray that you'll have…not the grim strength of gritting your teeth but the…strength God gives…that endures the unendurable and spills over into joy" (Col 1:11 TM). Hang in there. What God has in store for you is worth any price you have to pay!

The toughest times are those when everything you know about God *still* doesn't help you to get the results you want!

Those are the times when you learn about His *silence*.

Whenever God doesn't speak a word, He's teaching even in the stillness. He's allowing us to grow by *forcing* us to think, study, believe, and arrive at conclusions, while He stands by with a hushed smile and watchful eye.

Faith comes by *hearing*. Patience comes by *silence*.

Patience is what God gives us when things don't seem to be changing. It's His sedative for the troubled heart. It's the balm He rubs into our aching muscles when it feels like we're being stretched to breaking point.

Those are the times when the pain lasts so long that only *God* can supply the grace needed to sustain you.

Patience is just strength harnessed, power focused, and faith taking its time.

There are two groups mentioned in Hebrews, Chapter eleven. The first "Escaped... the sword" (v. 34), the second were "slain with the sword" (v. 37). God brought the first group *out*, and the second group *through*, but both "obtained a good report through faith" (Heb 11:39).

Faith is not always an instrument of change; sometimes it's a means of survival. It's perfected more when things *don't* change, than when they *do*.

You don't need faith for what you can *see* or have already *attained*. You need it when life makes no sense…when you can't explain why the pain won't stop…the job falls through…the marriage isn't working…the wicked prosper… the good die…the righteous suffer…and the kind receive no comfort.

Because we have limited perspective, we restrict our expectations of *who* God is and *what* He can do. We think the only good outcome is the one *we* want!

Instead, we must try to see Him at work in *whatever* comes our way, and trust Him, for He "causes *everything* to work together for the good of those who love God and are called according to his purpose" (Ro 8:28 NLT). Did you get that? *Everything!*

WebMD reports that people who *don't* attend church or have a strong faith in God: (1) have an average hospital stays *three times* longer than those who do; (2) are *fourteen times* more likely to die following surgery; (3) have a *forty-percent higher* death rate from heart disease and cancer; (4) have *twice* the number of strokes.

Today God's saying to you, "Do not throw away your confidence; it *will* be richly rewarded. You need to *persevere* so that when you have done the will of God, you will *receive* what he has promised" (Heb 10:35-36 NIV).

Whether God heals you through a doctor, or through divine intervention, *He alone* is the source of all healing. His word says; (a) "The Lord will guide you continually…keeping you healthy too" (Isa 58:11 NLT). *That's divine health.* (b) "The prayer of faith shall save the sick and the Lord will raise him up" (Jas 5:16). *That's divine healing.*

In The Old Testament, each Israeli family left Egypt through the door of their home, which had been sprinkled with *the blood* of a lamb, "And there was not one feeble person among their tribes" (Ps 105:37). That means when you're sick you have the *blood-bought privilege* of praying in the Name of Jesus, believing that when you do, His power will be released to heal you, set you free from crippling habits, and bring answers to your prayers.

One of history's greatest stories of *faith* is found in the Book of Joshua. Listen, "Joshua spoke to the Lord…so the sun stood still" (Jos 10:12-13 NKJV).

Joshua was fighting with everything he had, but there was one element he couldn't control – the sun. So he told God, "I'll do what I *can,* but I'm calling on You to do what I *can't.* Arrest the thing that controls the entire system!"

When you're running out of time and you need a 25th hour in your day, there's only one place to go – God! He can stop the sun and freeze the circumstances! He can give you time to regroup, develop a new strategy, and go on to win the battle.

In the 25th hour God allows you to redeem the time you've squandered attacking others and feeling sorry for yourself, when you should have been out fighting the enemy. Theologically, we'd call it *grace*; we don't get it because of our merits, we get it because of God's goodness. If you've ever had God do you a favor you didn't deserve – that's grace!

Listen, "There has been no day like that before it or after it" (Jos 10:14 NKJV). *Twenty-fifth hour people are different.* (1)They pray prayers that nobody's ever prayed before, because they believe "There is nothing is too hard for the Lord" (Je 32:17). (2) They remember their wasted years, and live with gratitude for the gift of a second chance. (3) They have a renewed sense of urgency and mission, because even though the clock had run out, God gave them *extra time* to come back and win the game.

It's not too late for you. Joshua's God is *your* God. Talk to Him – He's still in control!

7
THE BABY'S NOT DEAD!

On February 23, 1996, about four or five months into her pregnancy, Mary Clarke remembers, "I wasn't feeling well. I was having a hard time breathing, and was very dizzy."

Her doctor told her to come in immediately.

As the nurse examined her she said, "We should be able to hear the baby's heartbeat."

She tried for quite a while, but was unable to pick it up. When the doctor came into the room, the examining nurse asked him to try, and after ten or fifteen minutes without success, they decided to do an ultrasound.

In the ultrasound room the doctor still couldn't get a heart beat, so he called a colleague in to assist. But the second physician was also unable to hear it.

As this point the doctor told Mary and her husband, Ron, "The baby has died. I can't tell you why these things happen. I'm very sorry, but you'll have to be induced."

"Our hearts were broken. We'd lost our precious baby," Mary said.

A nurse took them to the birthing center and explained what would happen when they induced labor.

"As I was lying in bed," Mary says, "I prayed that God would watch over our baby until we could meet him or her in heaven."

Meanwhile, Mary's sister telephoned Pat Bailey, a woman from their church, and asked her to pray. When Pat got the call she said something startling, *"That baby's not dead. Tell them to double-check and get another opinion."*

So Ron and Mary talked to the doctor and asked him to do one more test before the procedure was performed. To appease them, he ordered one last ultrasound.

Back in the ultrasound room, a different nurse, who didn't know why the couple was there, began the ultrasound. A moment later she said matter-of-factly, "And there's the heartbeat!"

"Are you sure?" Mary asked.

The nurse replied, "The baby's heartbeat is

perfect, no problems."

Turning to the nurse from the birthing center, Mary saw that her jaw had dropped and her eyes were as round as saucers.

Then they called the doctor in to look at the monitor.

Utterly amazed he said, *"If I hadn't seen this, I wouldn't have believed it. This can't be the same baby I saw on the other ultrasound!"*

As a precaution Mary was admitted to Good Samaritan Hospital, where her doctor later told her, "I would like to give you an explanation for what just happened – but I have none. A diagnosis like this is always verified by a second doctor, but there are times when medical science can't explain everything. Sometimes the only explanation is that *God* intervened."

"I didn't need an explanation," Mary said, "I knew God had performed a miracle, and that was all I needed to know."

On August 22, 1996, James Andrew Clarke was born – a healthy, beautiful boy! The doctor who delivered him, and had seen his lifeless form on he ultrasound, told Mary and Ron, *"This baby's really special!"*

8
EMOTIONAL HEALING

My cardiologist tells me that rates for heart disease and cancer *soar dramatically* during the two years immediately following the loss of a loved one. He says it's because of the close correlation between our *emotions* and our *immune* systems.

When researchers at King's College, London, did a long-term study of fifty-seven breast cancer patients who'd undergone mastectomies, they found that seven out of ten with "a strong faith" were still alive *ten years later*, while four out of five who "felt hopeless" at the time of diagnosis, had *died*.

Good nutrition is critical to good health – you can literally eat your way into an early grave.

Physical exercise is essential too. My wife bought me a treadmill last year, because while I'm gaining in wisdom, I seem to be losing in elasticity! How about you?

But there's a *third* element – a *spiritual* one – that's vital to enjoying the "long life" God promised us (See Ps 91:16).

What are you doing to nourish yourself spiritually – to feed your soul?

Jude writes, "Dear friends, *build yourselves up in…faith…and pray in the Holy Spirit*" (Jude 1:20 NIV). Have you learned to do that?

Paul writes, "Now I commit you to God and to the word of his grace which can *build you up*" (Acts 20:32 NIV).

Job wrote, "I have treasured the words of his mouth more than my daily bread" (Job 23:12 NIV). If we ate even a small fraction *spiritually*, of what we eat *physically*, we'd all be spiritual giants!

Jeremiah wrote, "When your words came, I *ate* them; they were my joy and my heart's delight, for I bear your name" (Jer 15:16 NIV). How come we who bear the name of Christ can watch television an average of seven hours a day, (that's forty-nine hours a week, or *nine full years* in an average life span!) yet claim we just don't have *time* to read and pray?

Peter writes, "Crave pure spiritual milk, so that by it you may *grow up…*" (1 Pe 2:2 NIV). How come we crave money, success, material things, the love of another person, yet we have *no hunger* for the things of God?

His Word is the *source* of spiritual strength!

Jesus spent the *first* hours of each day alone with God. Why? Because He knew what was waiting for Him! He made deposits each morning, therefore, He could make *withdrawals* throughout the day. Until you've prayed, *what* do you have to draw on? Until you hear from God, *what* do you have to say?

"But," you say, "I've been hurt in the past, and now I'm afraid to open up and trust again."

I understand. By age twelve I'd been molested twice by a church youth leader. My father died when I was thirteen, leaving me with an "orphaned heart" that didn't heal until I was in my mid-forties. I walked through the fires of divorce, and tried to *medicate* the pain with work, drugs, travel, and accomplishments – but they only made things worse.

I was in the tunnel of depression so long, I thought I'd *never* come out on the other end.

Friends I thought would *always* be there, abandoned me.

That's when I discovered that if *people* give you either your significance and security, they can take them away again.

Those were painful discoveries, but I'm glad I made them. Today I can tell you with confidence that not only does Christ *have* the answer – He *is* the answer!

We *all* deal with depression from time to time!

After forty years in ministry I've discovered that it not only visits the lowly, but also the highly placed – including those *prominent* in God's service.

Solomon writes, "Anxiety in the heart of man causes depression" (Pr 12:25 NKJV).

Long-term depression drains your energy, distorts your reality, assaults your faith, and affects everybody around you. One in five of us suffer from it. It's responsible for more workplace absenteeism than diabetes and heart disease.

Poor health, environment, stress, fear, loneliness, guilt, and anger, can all cause depression.

And it's not just a modern-day disease. It

touched the lives of many Bible characters too.

David experienced it because of *unconfessed sin*. He said, "I am…severely broken…my strength fails…my loved ones…stand afar off" (Ps 38:8-11 NKJV).

Job was so depressed about his financial, personal, and family losses, that he cursed the day he was born (See Job 3-3).

When Jezebel threatened *Elijah*, he went through the "H.A.L.T." syndrome. He was *Hungry*; he stopped eating. *Angry*; he got mad at God and the world. *Lonely*; he left his servant and went off by himself. *Tired*; he collapsed.

But God had a prescription. (a) He changed his diet; (b) Told him to rest; (c) Let him know he wasn't alone; (d) Sent an angel to minister to him.

And those are *still* the steps out of depression!

David said, "The Lord…brought me up out of a horrible pit" (Ps 40:1-2 NKJV), and He can bring you out of your depression too!

When you isolate and shut down, it can lead to "*The Jericho Syndrome.*"

What's that?

Listen, "Jericho was tightly shut up…no one

went out and no one came in" (Jos 6:1 NIV).
You're on "emotional lockdown," afraid to reach
out, or let anybody in. You build a wall so that
you won't be hurt again.

Look out! That wall can *imprison* you, and
everybody else in your life. You can get married
in Jericho, say the vows, wear the dress,
exchange the rings, go on the honeymoon, and
still have the walls up. You think, "If he leaves,
I'm ready. I've got a bank account I didn't tell
him about, and a game plan in case things don't
work out."

Jesus said, "A man…is joined to his wife"
(Mt 19:5 NLT). But how can you be *joined* to
someone if you can't even be *reached* because of
a wall of bitterness, fear, and distrust?

It's time for an exorcism! You've got to drive
out the ghosts of yesterday if you're to have any
real hope for a future together.

Stop rehearsing your past and give it to the
Lord. He's the wall-toppling, communication –
restoring, esteem-building healer of broken
hearts and relationships. *He can help you to live
and love again.*

He says, "Don't keep going over old history…

I am about to do something brand-new" (Isa 43:18-9 TM).

Cremate your past – don't embalm it!

Dr. Harold Blumfield says: "Unresolved emotional pain wreaks havoc on your immune system, cardiac function, hormone levels, and other physical functions. We must make peace with our past because our lives may literally depend on it." Challenging words!

Here are *seven suggestions* to help you meet the challenge of making peace with your past:

(1) *Reframe It.* Ask yourself, "How did it make me stronger? What do I know now that I didn't know then?" Be a learner not a loser.

(2) *Break the Shackles of Shame.* Shame isn't feeling bad about what you've done, it's feeling bad about what you *are* – and that's lethal! When God created you in His image he said, "I like it! It's very good" (See Ge 1:31). Start agreeing with Him!

(3) *Arrest the Acid Drip of Regret.* Stop punishing yourself with the "if only's." David said, "Happy is the person whose sins are forgiven …whom the Lord does not consider guilty" (Ps 32:1-2 NCV). Forgive yourself – because God

has! When He sees you through the finished work of Calvary, you look better to Him than you do to yourself!

(4) *Move from Grief to Gain.* Healing takes time, so expect some anger, fear, and sadness. Don't deny them – they're part of the healing process. But don't adopt them either – know when it's time to move on. You can't walk backwards into the future, and the future God has for you holds more happiness than any past you can remember.

(5) *Practice Acceptance.* While working in the Congo as a missionary, Helen Roseveare was brutally raped. Later she wrote, "I must ask myself the question, 'Can I thank God for trusting me with this experience, even if He never tells me why?'" The secret of trust doesn't lie in having all the answers; it lies in accepting that God's got it all figured out. It's knowing in the midst of whatever *has* happened, *is* happening, or *will* happen – He's still in control! You can either fix your mind on that and determine to laugh again, or whine your way through life complaining that you never got a fair shake.

(6) *Get Out of the "Blame Game."* It's a waste

of time! When you blame *yourself*, you multiply your guilt, rivet yourself to the past, and further diminish your already plummeting self-esteem. When you blame *God*, you cut yourself off from your only source of power; doubt replaces trust, and you put down roots of bitterness that make you cynical. When you blame *others*, you enlarge the distance between them and you, and close the only option that works – forgiveness!

(7) *Bury the Past, or Live with Its Ghosts.* Rehashing old hurts is like watching the same movie over and over, hoping for a different ending. Learn from it and move on. You don't drown by falling into the water, you drown by staying there!

It's not enough to merely escape your past; its power must be broken, otherwise it'll hound you for the rest of your life. When you break away from something that continually tries to recapture you, it's *crucial* to get the victory over it, otherwise you can't move forward!

Jesus said, "I give unto you power…over *all* the power of the enemy" (Lk 10:19). Rise up in His Name today and say, "I refuse to have another relapse, another nightmare, another bout of low self-esteem, confusion, or turmoil, because the Scripture says, 'If the Son sets you free, you will be free indeed'" (Jn 8:36 NIV).

It's terrifying to think that something's over only to find out it's not!

But remember, it was *God* who permitted Pharaoh to pursue Israel when they left Egypt. Why? "That I may show these signs of Mine… that you may tell…your son…the mighty things I have done" (Ex 10:1-2 NKJV).

God wants you to know two things. *First*, the only power the past has over you, is the power *you give it.* Listen, "The Egyptians whom you see today, you shall see again no more forever" (Ex 14:13 NKJV). *Second*, your children don't have to repeat your mistakes. The curse is lifted. They can grow up under God's blessing.

God could have resolved the Israelites' dilemma some other way, but He takes us *through* The Red Sea so that when we get to the other side and look back, we'll see the enemy "dead on the seashore" (Ex 14:30). Then we'll know the battle is *truly* over!

9
A FATHER'S TESTIMONY

Here's one father's faith-building testimony of how his son was miraculously healed following an automobile accident.

"On April 17, 2000, my son Nathan was in a near-fatal car accident.

Investigators believe he lost control of the family *convertible* while trying to avoid a deer.

"Forty-five minutes later, Kevin Lindow, a young man with emergency medical skills, found Nathan at the scene of the crash and gave him assistance while someone called for help.

"When he arrived at the hospital Nathan was suffering from a broken leg, spinal cord damage, and numerous lacerations to his body. He was having difficulty breathing because of a collapsed lung.

"In order to stabilize him the doctors decided to drug-induce a coma.

"Nathan spent four days in that coma. Doctors at Marshfield Clinic estimated his odds for survival at about *one-percent*.

When they discontinued the drugs he didn't regain consciousness.

"That night I prayed and read the Bible to Nathan, repeating the words that Jesus said to Lazarus, 'Come forth.' I told him, 'You've got to fight. You've got to wake up.'

"The next morning he did. When he acknowledged me later that afternoon we were beside ourselves with joy.

"But his spinal cord damage was still of major concern.

"He had sustained a fracture in the C-4 vertebrae in his neck – the same section that actor *Christopher Reeve* injured several years ago.

Because Nathan was in immediate danger of full or partial paralysis, his doctor gave him a protective collar to help prevent further separation of the vertebrae.

"Nathan had always made it a practice to read his Bible and pray before going to bed. For two weeks he prayed each night for healing.

"One night as he was falling asleep he

noticed "a popping sound" in his neck.

"The next morning physicians performed *three sets* of X-rays to see if the vertebrae were continuing to separate.

Instead, the X-rays showed that they had *fused back together!*

"The medical team was stunned. There was no human explanation!

"Three months after the accident, doctors cleared Nathan to resume his participation in athletics, including football, wrestling, and track and field."

10
WHERE ARE THE NINE?

This may surprise you, but I believe the most important decision we make on a day-to-day basis, is our choice of *attitude*.

It affects our mental, emotional, spiritual, and physical well-being.

It either keeps us moving forward, or cripples our progress. It fuels our fire, or assaults our hope. When our attitude is right, no barrier is too high, no valley too deep, no dream too extreme, and no challenge too great.

Yet we spend more time worrying about what *can't* be changed, than we do giving attention to the one thing that can – *our attitude*.

Did you hear about the woman and her daughter who went Christmas shopping?

The crowds were awful. They had to skip lunch because the mother was on a tight schedule. She was tired, irritable, and her feet hurt. As they left the last store, she turmed to her daughter and said, "Did you see the nasty look that salesman gave me?"

Her daughter replied, "He didn't *give* it to you, Mom, you already *had* it when you came in!"

You can't control the beauty of your face, but you can choose the expression on it. You can't control life's difficult moments, but you can choose how you respond to them. You can't control the negative atmosphere in the world around you, but you can choose the atmosphere in your own mind.

After being brutalized in Nazi concentration camps, Viktor Frankl wrote, "The last and greatest of all freedoms, *is the right to choose one's attitude* in any given circumstance."

That right can never be *taken* from you – *it can only be surrendered!*

That's what Paul meant when he wrote, "I have learned *the secret* of being content in any and every situation" (Php 4:12 NIV).

And what was his secret? Listen, "Whatever is *true*, whatever is *noble*, whatever is *right*, whatever is *pure*, whatever is *lovely*, whatever is *admirable* – if anything is excellent or praisewor-thy – *think* about such things…and the God of *peace* will be with you" (Php 4:8-9 NIV).

Your attitude doesn't run on automatic pilot. You've got to constantly correct it and feed it the right thoughts.

Trust is an attitude.

Listen, "The Lord's unfailing love surrounds the man who trusts in him" (Ps 32:10 NIV). Instead of trying to control things by rolling up our sleeves and mentally slugging it out, trust hands everything over to God, confident that He'll take care of it.

I once saw a humorous poster that read, *Who says worry doesn't work? Most of the things I worry about never happen!*

Try remembering what you worried about this time last year – or even last week! Can you?

Jesus said, "In this world you will have trou-ble. But take heart! I have overcome the world" (Jn 16:33 NIV). What happens to us doesn't hurt us half as much as our *perception* of it, and our *attitude* towards it.

What qualifies as worry?

Anything that drains your tank of joy…anything you can't change…anything you're not responsible for…anything you're unable to control…anything that frightens and torments you…anything that keeps you awake when you should be asleep.

All that baggage needs to be transferred from your *worry* list to your *prayer* list.

Listen, "Throw the whole weight of your anxieties on him, for you are his personal concern" (1 Pe 5:7 Phillips). Give your worries one-by-one to God! The more you *practice* doing this, the more exciting your walk with Him will become. You'll be amazed how easily *He* handles the things that overwhelm *you*.

Gratitude is also an attitude.

David writes, "O give thanks unto the Lord, for he is good; for his mercy endureth forever. Let the redeemed of the Lord say so, whom he hath redeemed from the hand of the enemy" (Ps 107:1-2). Again he says, "I will bless the Lord at all times; his praise shall continually be in my mouth" (Ps 34:1).

Notice the words, "I *will* bless the Lord at all times." It wasn't an impulse or reaction to circumstances, it was a *choice* he made each day!

When Jesus healed ten lepers but only one returned to give thanks, He asked him, "Were there not ten cleansed? but where are the *nine*?" (Lk 17:17). Then He said to the man, "Arise, go thy way; thy faith hath made thee *whole*" (Lk 17:19).

Note that while all ten received *healing*, the one who returned to give thanks was also made *whole*. What he received was not only *physical*, it was *emotional*, and *spiritual* as well.

In Luke, Chapter thirteen, Jesus healed a woman who'd been chronically ill for eighteen years. "He touched her, and instantly she could stand straight. How she praised and thanked God!" (Lk 13:13 LB).

When God straightens you up, make sure you glorify Him and nobody else! He may use others as instruments, but He *alone* is the source.

And be prepared – when you start glorifying God because of what he's done, some folks won't like it. As long as this woman still needed their help, the people around her had no problem. But when Jesus set her free and she began praising Him openly, they couldn't handle it. They wanted to throw her out of their church. Sound familiar?

How would *you* have reacted if you'd been ill for eighteen years and Jesus suddenly made you whole? People fall all over themselves about getting a prize on a television game show. When their team wins, they scream and hug total strangers, and the world thinks it's okay. But show a little emotion because of what *God* has done in your life and they'll brand you a fanatic. No problem; it's easier to cool down a fanatic than it is to warm up a corpse!

So again I ask – how would you have reacted?

You see, your *praise* is related to your former pain; the greater the *pain*, the greater the praise. Until you've been bound, you'll never know how good it feels to be free! Until you've walked in somebody else's shoes, you won't understand why they're dancing in them. Jesus said, "When you've received much, you'll love much" (Lk 7:47 para).

So what are you going to do?

Do what she did! Keep your rhythm and let Jesus deal with the critics. *While she was glorifying Him, He was dealing with them.* That's how it works! While you're praising God, He's fighting for you. While you're exalting His name, His angels are coming into your hospital room, or surrounding your loved one who's in danger, or going before you to open doors.

If people get upset when you praise the Lord, that's *their* problem! There'll always be critics. There may even be one in your house, criticizing you for praising God in the shower; or at work, mocking you for giving thanks before you eat lunch.

Pay them no attention – just keep praising God regardless of the background noise.

If your friends don't like you to praise God, don't change your praise – change your friends!

Whether you shout, whisper, or fall on your face, God is worthy to be praised. He commands it! He delights in it! He *dwells* in it!

You say, "What's the big deal about praise?" (1) It draws people closer together. (2) It focuses your attention on the problem-solver, instead of the problem. (3) It changes the climate around you, driving out fear and negativity and creating an atmosphere in which God can move. (4) It brings God's presence into your situation, and *that* spells victory every time!

11
METHODS OF HEALING

God has *many* methods of healing. Naaman the leper was cleansed by dipping seven times in the river Jordan. A woman who was hemorrhaging severely just touched the hem of Jesus' garment, and immediately was healed. On another occasion Jesus rubbed clay on a blind man's eyes and his sight was restored.

You can't dictate to God!

People who are divinely healed tend to be those who approach God with an *open heart*, saying, "Lord, Your Word says You'll heal me. I'm willing to do *anything* You tell me. I don't care *how* You do it, or *who* You use, just do it!"

Here are some methods God uses to bring healing to us:

(1) *Praying in faith.* You can only exercise faith to be healed when you know that God's already promised it. Your faith must be lined up

with His Word, otherwise you'll get nowhere.

If you were taught that you can "glorify God" more in sickness than by being healed, you'll have a problem.

If sickness glorifies God, then Jesus *robbed* God of that glory, by healing "all that were oppressed." His successor, The Holy Spirit, who was sent to continue what Jesus had begun, *also* robbed God of the glory by healing all the people in the streets of Jerusalem. And Paul did the *same* when he healed all that were sick on the island of Melita.

God is glorified when we exercise faith, persevere, rejoice, and maintain our confidence in Him during times of sickness. But He is not the author of sickness. The Bible says He heals "all our diseases" (Ps 103:3 NIV).

Listen, "Jesus Christ is the same yesterday and today and forever" (Heb 13:8 NIV). That means what He *was* He still *is*; what He *did* He still *does*; what He *said* He still *says*.

But you must believe His Word, for "Without faith it is impossible to please God, because anyone who comes to him *must* believe…that he rewards those who earnestly seek him" (Heb 11:6 NIV).

(2) *Confessing The Word.* One day Jesus said to His disciples, "Have faith in God...I tell you the truth, if anyone *says* to this mountain, 'Go, throw yourself into the sea,' and does not doubt in his heart but believes what he *says* will happen, it will be done for him. Therefore I tell you, whatever you *ask* for in prayer, believe that you have received it, and it will be yours" (Mk 11:23-24 NIV).

A negative confession will always *lower* your faith to the level of that confession. What you confess controls you. If it's negative it'll imprison you in your circumstances. But a faith-filled confession will set you free.

Solomon said "You are snared [trapped] by the words of your mouth" (Pr 6:2 NKJV). When you doubt God's Word by entertaining thoughts that are contrary to what He says, you shut His power out, and allow the enemy to come in.

Don't be fragmented; stop *reading* one thing and *saying* another! Your words, thoughts, and actions must all be in sync.

Furthermore, sickness becomes more dominant when you confess the testimony of your *senses*. Feelings and appearances have *no place* in the realm of faith.

Confessing disease is like signing for a package that's just been delivered to your door. Satan then has the receipt showing that you've *accepted* it! The Bible says, "Do not give the devil a foothold" (Eph 4:27 NIV).

You say, "But my feelings keep changing. I'm susceptible to the opinions of those around me."

God has given you the power to "take captive every thought" (2 Co 10:5 NIV). Either you control your thoughts or they control you!

Soak yourself in Scripture. Get into agreement with God. Refuse to say anything except what His Word proclaims.

(3) *Using the name of Jesus.* Listen: "*In my name*...they will place their hands on sick people, and they will get well" (Mk 16:17-18 NIV). At the cross Jesus defeated Satan, the source of sickness, fear, addiction, and anything else that robs you of God's best.

So each time you ask in the name of *Jesus*, you repeat the name of the *victor*, into the ears of Satan the *vanquished*, and he has to leave. He has no choice!

Just as a policemen is empowered by the government he represents, so Jesus has empowered you. Listen: "I give you power...over *all* the power of the enemy" (Lk 10:19). Today that power is yours! Use it!

(4) *The laying on of hands.* Listen, "He called his twelve disciples to him and gave them authority to...heal every disease and sickness" (Mt 10:1 NIV). Before Jesus left the earth He said: (a) "As my father hath sent me, even so send I you" (Jn 20:21). (b) "The works that I do shall [ye] do also" (Jn 14:2). (c) "They shall lay hands on the sick and they shall recover" (Mk 16:18).

How wonderful – your hands can be *His* healing hands extended to others. He's the source, you're the conduit through which His power flows!

And it's not limited to those in ministry. It's promised to "them that believe" (Mk 16:17). Go ahead, lay hands on your loved ones, speak the Name of Jesus over them, and expect them to recover.

(5) *Fasting.* One day Jesus' disciples encountered a boy who was so controlled by evil spir-

its, that he'd tried *repeatedly* to take his own life. When the disciples attempted to cast these spirits out, they got nowhere. Jesus stepped in and said, "I command you, come out of him and never enter him again" (Mk 9:25 NIV). The boy was immediately set free.

When the disciples asked Jesus why they weren't able to cast the spirits out, Jesus replied, "This kind can come out by nothing but by prayer and *fasting*" (Mk 9:29 NKJV).

Those who experience great demonstrations of God's healing power, are people who invariably give themselves to prayer - and fasting.

Why? Because fasting: (a) sharpens your spiritual focus; (b) brings your flesh into subjection; (c) demonstrates a hunger that God always responds to.

While preaching a crusade in the Philippines, I gave an invitation to those who were sick to come forward.

There were about twenty-thousand people in the audience, and hundreds of them surged toward me. It was like a sea of human suffering, and I felt overwhelmed. I laid hands on them and prayed, but nothing seemed to happen.

I felt powerless.

Heartsick I returned to my tiny motel room, fell on my knees and prayed, "Lord, I *never* want to be in that position again. Unless You move tomorrow night, I don't want to go to church, I don't want to preach, and I sure don't want to lay hands on anybody."

I fasted and prayed the following day, saturating my mind with God's promises concerning healing, and seeking for a fresh in-filling of His Spirit. He graciously visited me.

That night I went to church with a sense of faith I'd never known before.

Again when the invitation for prayer was given, hundreds came forward.

The first lady I laid hands on had a huge goiter, and I watched in amazement as it shrunk. Another man who had come on crutches, threw them away and started dancing wildly. The following day some people came to my room, bringing a man I'd prayed for the night before. They told me, "He was blind, but now he can see clearly."

I'm not sure *why* healings take place so freely in foreign countries where people have so little.

Perhaps it's because they've nothing *but* God, or maybe it's because their faith is so simple.

One thing I do know for sure, I saw a demonstration of God's healing power that night that I've never seen before or since. I "tapped into it" when I decided to *fast*, and call from the depths of my being to the God who said, "You will seek me and find me, when you seek me with *all* your heart" (Jer 29:12).

(6) *Prayer cloths*. Listen, "God did extraordinary miracles through Paul…handkerchiefs and aprons that had touched him were taken to the sick and their illnesses were cured" (Acts 19:11-12 NIV).

Last year in Belfast, Northern Ireland, the brother of a policeman who was dying of cancer, came into Metropolitan Tabernacle and requested a "prayer cloth." Pastor Jim McConnell prayed over the cloth during the Sunday evening service, anointed it with oil, and the man gave it to his brother.

Not being a believer, his brother didn't understand that it was simply *a point of contact* through which God's healing power is transferred to those who are sick.

He put the cloth in his pocket, probably thinking, "What have I got to lose?"

A week later, to everybody's astonishment, his oncologist pronounced him cancer free!

(7) *Walking in obedience.* God can't bless you beyond your last act of disobedience. Stop and take inventory. What has He told you to do that you're still not doing?

He told His people, "If you pay attention to these laws and are careful to follow them... the Lord will keep you free from every disease" (Dt 7:12&15 NIV). John writes, "We have confidence before God and receive from him *anything* we ask, because we *obey* his commandments and do what *pleases* him" (1 Jn 3:22 NIV).

Here are some areas of disobedience that may be hindering your healing:

(a) *Unforgiveness:* "When you stand praying, if you hold anything against anyone, forgive him, so that your Father in heaven may forgive you your sins" (Mk 11:25 NIV). (b) *Robbing God:* "You are under a curse...because you are robbing me. Bring the whole tithe into the storehouse" (Mal 3:9-10 NIV). (c) *Secret sin:* "If I regard iniquity in my heart the Lord will not hear me" (Ps 66:18). (d) *Ignoring God's principles:* "Then they will call on me but I will not answer; they will look for me but will not find me...since they would not accept my advice and spurned my rebuke" (Pr 1:28-29 NIV). (e) *Indifference toward others:* "If a man shuts his ears to the cry of the poor, he too will cry out and not be answered" (Pr 21:13 NIV). (f) *Stubbornness:* "When I called, they did not listen; so when they called, I would not listen, says the Lord" (Zac 7:13). (g) *Instability:* "When he asks, he must *believe* and not *doubt*, because he who doubts is like a wave of the sea, blown and tossed by the wind. That man should not think he will receive anything from the Lord; he is a double-minded man, unstable in all he does" (Jas 1:6-8 NIV). (h) *Self-indulgence:* "When you ask, you do not receive, because you ask with wrong motives, that you may spend what you get on your pleasures" (Jas 4:3 NIV). (i) *Failure to use wisdom:* "The heart of the discerning acquires acknowledge; and the ears of the wise seek it out" (Pr 18:15 NIV). Unhealthy lifestyle habits cannot only *make* you sick, they *keep* you that way.

A well known Bible teacher told some friends of mine that after suffering for years from stomach trouble, he prayed for healing but didn't receive it. When he asked God what the problem was, God told him to *quit drinking so much coffee.* He did, and he hasn't had an attack since.

Sixty percent of America is fighting obesity. Pharmaceutical companies are actually trying to produce a pill that will "cure it" while allowing us to eat *what* we want, as *often* as we want, and as *much* as we want.

One of my dearest friends experienced total kidney failure, and spent several years on dialysis until God providentially turned up a kidney donor.

Why did his kidneys fail?

He believes part of the reason was this: as a young man overseas in the military, his sergeant instructed him to be sure to always add purifying tablets to his canteen of drinking water. But this process took several hours, and what nineteen-year-old wants to wait that long? So instead of drinking water, he developed the habit of drinking six or eight cans of Coca Cola every day. (I'm told each can contains about *ten* teaspoons of sugar!).

Today when this man preaches about healing, he tells people, "Don't just use *faith* to be healed, use *wisdom* and stay healthy."

If you've got a family predisposition towards obesity, thyroid problems, or other genetic disorders, God understands, and He can heal you. But if you're a couch potato who clogs your arteries with junk food and never exercises, don't blame Him when the machine breaks down.

Your body is a temple, and as such, it should be a place of *order*, where God is *glorified*.

12
PRAYERS FOR HEALING

No book about healing would be complete without some scripturally-based prayers for you to pray when you need God's healing touch. On the following pages, you'll find four you can use.

Prayer 1
Protection from Sickness and Disease

"Because you have made the Lord...even the
Most High your dwelling place, no evil shall befall
you, nor shall any plague come near your dwelling;
for He shall give His angels charge over you,
to keep you in all your ways."
Psalm 91:9-11 NKJV

Lord, I rejoice that all authority has been given to You in heaven and on earth (Mt 28:18). No principality or power, no human institution or invention, no infirmity or illness can prevail against You (Eph 1:21). I rejoice also that You have given your disciples authority to heal sickness (Lk 9:1-2).

From the common cold to terminal cancer, I take authority over the spirit of infirmity, and forbid it to prevail against me (Lk 13:11). I stand on Your Word which says, no evil shall befall me, nor shall any plague come near my dwelling. Dispatch Your angels to encamp around about me, and protect me from all harm" (Ps 91:9-11).

Your Word says You "Will bless the righteous; With favor You will surround him as with a *shield*" (Ps 5:12 NKJV). I ask that no disease would come near me; that the magnitude of Your presence around me be so great that *nothing* will be able to touch me, except that which comes from You.

Because my body is the temple of the Holy Spirit (1 Co 3:16-17), steer me away from destructive habits that make me vulnerable to weakness and infirmity. I want to worship you, body, soul, and spirit.

May the hedge of protection You have placed around me serve as a testimony to others of Your power, Your protection, and Your love. In Christ's Name. AMEN.

PRAYER 2
Physical Healing

*"Surely He has borne our griefs and carried our
"sorrows… And by His stripes we are healed."*
Isaiah 53:4-5 NKJV

Lord, I come before You in the Name of Jesus, knowing that You hear my prayer and care about my needs. Your love is stronger than my sin. Your faithfulness is greater than my suffering. Your power is mightier than my sickness. Your are *Jehovah Rapha*, the Lord who heals me (Ex 15:26).

Cause Your creative, life-giving power, to course throughout my body, making me completely whole again. Your Word says You have borne my griefs and carried my sorrows…and by Your stripes I am *healed* (Isa 53: 4-5).

It also says, "Confess your trespasses to one another, and pray for one another, that you may be healed" (Jas 5:16 NKJV). Examine my heart. Convict me. Purge me of any sin that hinders the flow of Your healing power.

Lord, everyone who touched You during

Your earthly ministry was made whole, and You have not changed. Right *now* I reach out and touch the hem of Your garment, believing that I shall be made whole (Mk 5:27-29).

I place my complete confidence in Your love, Your faithfulness, and Your power to overcome sickness and disorder in my life.

I rejoice in advance as I anticipate Your intervention in my situation. I cast all my care upon You, because I know You care for me. (1 Pe 5:7). In Christ's Name. AMEN.

PRAYER 3
RECOVERY FROM SURGERY

"About this time, Hezekiah got sick and was almost dead. He prayed, and the Lord gave him a sign that he would recover."
2 Chronicles 32:24 CEV

Lord, I come to You in the Name of Jesus, thanking You for the expertise You have given men and women in the medical profession, enabling them to be instruments of Your healing. All knowledge and skill begins *with* You and results *from* You. "Every good gift…is from above, and comes down from the Father" (Jas 1:17).

Just as Hezekiah prayed and You gave him a sign that he would recover, so I ask You to grant me complete recovery.

Please provide a sign to show those around me that You are intimately involved in my life, and in their lives as well. May my recovery impress doctors, nurses, technicians, medical personnel, visitors, and friends, in such a way that they will know they have seen the hand of the Lord.

Use my recovery as an opportunity to strengthen me spiritually. Fill my room with songs of praise. Avert my eyes from television to the riches of Your Word. Stir my spirit so that I can be an intercessor for others.

I choose to put on the garment of praise instead of the spirit of heaviness (Isa 61:3). I choose to see the good You are working in my life as a result of my recuperation (See Ro 5:3-5).

When my healing is complete, give me words for those around me concerning Your saving and healing power. In every way may my recovery bring glory to You. In Christ's Name. AMEN.

PRAYER 4
EMOTIONAL HEALING

"But to you who fear my name, the Sun of Righteousness will rise with healing in his wings."
Malachi 4:2 CEV

Lord, I choose to remember all the benefits You have given me. You forgive all my sins and heal all my diseases. You rescue me from all danger. You crown me with love and compassion. You satisfy my desires with good things, so that I am renewed in every way (See Ps 103:2-5).

Today I lay my life before You, seeking Your redeeming, renewing touch. You said, "Take my yoke upon you and learn from Me, for I am gentle and lowly in heart, and you will find rest for your souls [emotions]. For My yoke is easy and My burden is light" (Mt 11:29-30 NKJV). I release to You my burdens, my hurts, discouragement, hopelessness, anger, and despair.

You shed Your blood on the cross, not only for my forgiveness and physical healing, but also for my emotional well-being (See Mt 8:16-17).

Your Word declares that You heal the brokenhearted and bind up their wounds (See Ps 147:3). Lord, bind up my wounds. Recreate them into reminders of Your redeeming love.

Instead of simply erasing the memory, give me eyes to see it through your grace. Show me that in my darkest hours You were there – strengthening and encouraging me to go on; walking beside me, ensuring that I wouldn't experience more heartache than I could endure (See 1 Co 10:13).

No matter how dark the night may be, I know Your mercies are new every morning. Sun of Righteousness, shine the light of Your love into every corner of my life. Release me from this pain so that I can rejoice in You. Apply the oil of joy to my broken heart. Redeem my past, and use it to mold me into the person You designed me to be. In Christ's Name. AMEN.

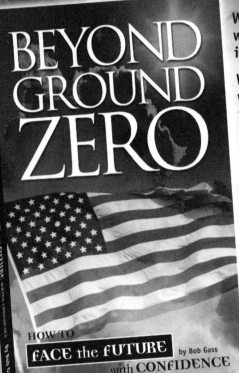

Write today...
AND GET YOUR COPY!

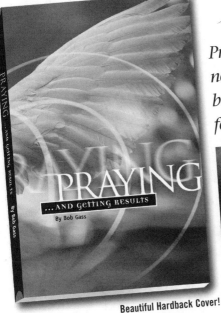

Praying is not for God's benefit, it is for yours!

Author, Bob Gass

Beautiful Hardback Cover!

Praying And Getting Results Praying is not for God's benefit, it is for yours! You don't need to understand it anymore than you need to understand electricity, in order to enjoy its benefits. Just acknowledge its potential, plug in, and start getting results! Prayer can change everything in your life for the better. Everything! Read this book and find out how.